Concert and Contest COLLECTION

Edited MAN

for

Bb TENOR SAXOPHONE with piano accompaniment

CONTENTS

RUBANK®

HAL•LEONARD®
CORPORATION
7777 W. BLUEMOUND RD. P.O. BOX 13819 MILWAUKEE, WI 53213

Contradance

W. A. MOZART
Transcribed by H. Voxman

Sinfonia
(Arioso)
from Cantata No. 156*

J. S. BACH
Transcribed by H. Voxman

* This Cantata was composed by Bach ca. 1730. The original scoring of the Sinfonia is for solo oboe, strings, and continuo. The eighth-note accompaniment figures (treble) should probably be played quasi pizzicato. Bach also used this melody in a more elaborate version in his F minor Concerto for clavier.

Allegretto

A. ARENSKY
Transcribed by H. Voxman

Valse Nouvelle
from Album for the Young

P. TCHAIKOVSKY, Op. 39, No. 8
Transcribed by H. Voxman

Menuetto and Presto
from Trio V

F. J. HAYDN
Transcribed by H. Voxman

Presto D.C. al Fine
(with repeats)

Two Little Tales

E. DESPORTES
Transcribed by H. Voxman

I - SENTIMENTAL

II – GAY

The Old Castle
from Pictures at an Exhibition

M. MUSSORGSKY
Transcribed by H. Voxman

Pièce in G Minor

GABRIEL PIERNÉ, Op. 5
Edited by H. Voxman

Première Étude de Concours

A. S. PETIT
Edited by H. Voxman

Prelude and Allegro

LEROY OSTRANSKY

Novelette

GEORGES SPORCK
Edited by H. Voxman

First Concertino

GEORGES GUILHAUD
Transcribed by H. Voxman

Adagio and Allegro
(from Sonata No. 6 for Violin & Keyboard)

G. F. HANDEL
Transcribed by H. Voxman